W9-CQG-479

IN THE SILENCE ABSENCE MAKES

ESSENTIAL POETS SERIES 129

ONTARIO ARTS COUNCIL
CONSEIL DES ARTS DE L'ONTARIO

Guernica Editions Inc. acknowledges the support
of The Canada Council for the Arts.
Guernica Editions Inc. acknowledges the support
of the Ontario Arts Council.
Guernica Editions Inc. acknowledges the Government of Ontario
through the Ontario Media Development
Corporations Ontario Book Initiative.
Guernica Editions Inc. acknowledges the financial support of the
Government of Canada through the Book Publishing
Industry Development Program (BPIDP).

HALLI VILLEGAS

IN THE SILENCE

ABSENCE MAKES

GUERNICA

TORONTO···BUFFALO···CHICAGO···LANCASTER (U.K.)
2004

Antonio D'Alfonso, editor
Guernica Editions Inc.
P.O. Box 117, Station P, Toronto (ON), Canada M5S 2S6
2250 Military Road, Tonawanda, N.Y. 14150-6000 U.S.A.

Distributors:
University of Toronto Press Distribution,
5201 Dufferin Street, Toronto, (ON), Canada M3H 5T8
Gazelle Book Services, White Cross Mills, High Town, Lancaster LA1 1XS U.K.
Independent Publishers Group,
814 N. Franklin Street, Chicago, Il. 60610 U.S.A.

First edition.
Printed in Canada.

Legal Deposit — First Quarter
National Library of Canada
Library of Congress Catalog Card Number: 2003114599

National Library of Canada Cataloguing in Publication
Villegas, Halli
In the silence absence makes / Halli Villegas.
(Essential poets series ; 129)
Poems.
ISBN 1-55071-198-9
I. Title. II. Series.
PS8593.I3894I5 2004   C811'.6 C2003-906556-1

Acknowledgements

Thank you to Allan Briesmaster, Chris Doda, Priscila Uppal, Tim Hanna, Tracy Carbert, Sue Bowness, Robin Blackburn, Keith Daniels and Ben McCarthy for support during this book's growing pains.

Thank you to my family, especially my sisters who shared their girlhood with me. "The sisters are doin' for themselves!"

Thank you to David for making my life one long writers retreat.

Special thanks to my friend and editor the inestimable Antonio D'Alfonso.

For the girls

What I heard was but the limpid melody of children at play, nothing but that . . . then I knew that the hopelessly poignant thing was not Lolita's absence from my side, but the absence of her voice from that concord.

Vladimir Nabokov, *Lolita*

There is a beauty mark
Below her left eye
A small scar on her chin
From a fall when she was four

After her bath
When her hair
Is clean dry combed
Stray stands float
Filaments of light
Human halo

Her first recital
Net caught with stars
Around her waist

When she glides centre stage
The other little girls
Seem to recede

She's alone aglow
Her small bones chime
I am sublime

She likes to play games – Clue
Life Sorry –
Is still obsessed with horses
Keeps a picture of her cat
Beside her pink and white bed

Above her bed
She has stuck stars
That glow in the dark
So the last thing
She sees at night
Her constant sky
Stars ordered to her wish

She peoples her dollhouse
With plastic animals
Instead of the stiff figures provided
Plans to become a vet
Live on a farm someday

She refuses to go to the zoo
She knows the animals there
Dream of home

She presses
Four leaf clovers
Between pages

Watches the sky
For a star
To loose its hold

Blows out
The candles
On her cake

In infinite hope

When she was eight
She made her best friend
Eat a green crayon
Discovered a power in cruelty
That scared her

She became dreamy and distant
To avoid

Recess the girls
Play war with the boys
Chasing calling cooties
As the bell rings
Them back to class

In her science class
Is a cage with cocoons
She thinks she can see
Through the white sacs
A dark pulse
Something dormant but alive

In class she watches a movie
A lizard's tongue
Takes a newly hatched butterfly
Just as it first spreads wet wings
To test them

She plays the flute
In the school band
Her thin silver song
Seems to hang about
Her heels

She and her friends
Make wings
Schoolroom newsprint
And untwisted wire hangers

Late fall –
Their uniform skirts
Hang below winter coats
But still bare knees
Marred with mud

They jump from bleachers
In the park
Land in leaves
Wet with imminent winter

Hoarse voiced
Smelling of earth
They fly
Until it is dark

In the mirror
She paints her lips
With Snow Silver Rose
Finishes off with
Bubblegum scented gloss

Sticky plump
Sweet smelling lips
Of the not yet
Been kissed

It is spring
Her uniform skirt
Is too short
Her legs
Have grown like grass

She sometimes planned
To runaway

When her mother made her mad
Her life intolerable because of
Dishes or homework

She'd pack a bag take an apple
Hide in the neighbor's garage

But when the street lights came on
She always came home
Where her family
Was just sitting down
To dinner

In winter
She makes snow angels
On the lawn

White wings
Frozen in flight

They fly further
Then she can see

In summer she and her friends
Are allowed to camp out
In the backyard
Pup tent flashlights
Box of cookies
Light left on in the kitchen
Just in case

They tell ghost stories
The scariest things
They can imagine

Tinny tune
Neighborhood ice cream man
Children swarm
Hard earned coins clutched

She stands back
Her cherry chip cone
Has been free
Since she was seven

Pressure of the ice cream man's
Finger on the knob of her wrist
As he hands it to her

She and her mother
Plant flowers
Along the fence
Each new bloom color
Catches her

She calls out
As she bends over
The blossoms

Fresh strawberries
Stain her lips tongue
Finger tips

When she bites
Into another
The gap where she's lost
A baby tooth
Visible for a moment

So hot she and her friend
Run through the sprinklers
Curve of their tummies
In shiny swimsuits
Wet hair sends a halo
Of droplets
Each screaming pass

The same car has driven
By the house unnoticed
Three times now

Long shadows on the lawn
Her bike left out
Though she's been told
A million times

Her jump rope:
Coiled snake
Dead on the path

Logged on
He punches in Lolita
Little girls in knee socks
And nothing else
Tumble onto his screen

He seeks them
Where they can't hide

He lights one cigarette
After another
Waiting for the girls
To let out of school
Released butterflies
He watches

The cigarette butts
Thick strewn around the tree
May be a clue

I cannot find
The one I want
Among these girls

He knows that he has
A trustworthy face
The eyes alone
Might give something away
He distracts with joking laughter
Pleas for help
Only they can provide

He does not believe
In luck
Only opportunity

He does not
Make wishes
Come true

He paces the room
Flips from channel to channel
Even nicotine does not
Make the connections clear tonight

He is afraid
He will make a mistake

He sleepwalks her
From her father's home
Wherever he wakes her
It will not be
In her own bed

How many times
Did we tell her
After a nightmare
That it was just a dream

Birds rise from the trees
In a hornet black swarm
Crying too late
Too late
Into the simple summer sky

His step on the stair

Her legs leaden
Chest stretched
With fear's heartbeat
Urgency in her bladder
Prays it will not break

Was it someone she knew
What about the family friend
Who when drunk confessed to her
He had imagined her parents dead
She and her sister orphaned
Only him to turn to

His over hearty hugs
Fingers like the ones
That can't resist
Brushing the velvety glow
Of butterfly wings
Even when they know
Their touch will ruin
What they desire

Girls grow on trees
Can be plucked at will
Fed upon til full
Thrown out
With the rest of the waste

The forest behind her house
Is filled with bones
The cadaver dogs
Sigh into the leaves
At the base of the trees
Searching

She sinks soundlessly
Into the swamp
He has chosen for her

Her potential
What she might have been
Will not stay under

Buoyed she surfaces

Forgotten at the bottom
Of the closet
Her doll stares into the dark
Shakes hands endlessly
With air

Left behind
Her first purse
Hangs in the hall

In it her house key
Five dollar allowance
Invitation from her friend
To a birthday party
Next week

On the pole
Whose surface
Is already silvered with staples
Enlarged in black and white
Grainy blur of a girl
Who up close
Dissolves into pixels
Might be a sister
A daughter
Only thing certain
Are the words
Written in red:
Have you seen this girl

Sometimes someone
Saw something
The girl a shadow
Too brief a glance
To be sure

It might have been her

Who sees that she's fed
Where is she put to bed
What stars reel above her head

We have to ask:
How old is she
What was she wearing
Where was she
Last seen

Her cat will not go in her room
Stops at the bedroom door
Expectant only for a moment
Then goes into the garden
Kills a bird
Leaves it on the back steps
Before disappearing for good

The entire class went to the assembly
Was given the handouts
Who not to talk to
What to do
How to call for help
She was in the third row

We just don't know
What more we can do

The stranger
Is not strange
No gruesome ogre
Misshapen beast
A seamless stake
In the topside world

Only his heart
Is fairy tale true
Brutal and bloody
As Bluebeard's
Locked room

What eyes watch
In this neighborhood
What do they see

May be in the company of a white male
Age approximately twenty-seven
Average height
Average weight
Clean shaven

May not be

On the front porch
Eyed by a stuffed bear
With rain matted fur
A letter whose words have run
Washed out flowers

The family is not
At home

There's a girl sleeping
In the empty lot
Why don't the flies
Wake her

In her class photo
She is in the front row
But she turned her head
To watch a robin
Settle on the window ledge

She is just a streak of light
Among the other children

She knows where she is
She is on her way home
The air is filled with butterflies

With every beat
Of their fragile wings
The world shifts

Printed in
April 2004
at Gauvin Press Ltd., Gatineau, Québec